SQL FOR BEGINNERS

A SIMPLIFIED GUIDE TO MANAGING, ANALYZING, AND MANIPULATING DATA EASILY

AHMET NESELI

SQL For Beginners: A Simplified Guide to Managing, Analyzing, and Manipulating Data Easily

Copyright © 2024 Ahmet Neseli

For permission requests, please contact the author at ahmetneseli@gmail.com.

Disclaimer:

The information contained in this book is provided for educational purposes only. While every effort has been made to ensure accuracy, the author and publisher assume no responsibility for errors or omissions or for damages resulting from the use of the information herein. Always consult a qualified professional for specific guidance related to your needs.

TABLE OF CONTENTS

TABLE OF CONTENTS

1

INTRODUCTION TO SQL

1.1 What is SQL?

SQL (Structured Query Language) is a domain-specific language used to interact with relational databases. It allows users to:

• Retrieve, manipulate, and query data stored in databases.

• Define the structure of data (e.g., creating tables).

• Control access to the database through user permissions.

• Analyze data for reporting and decision-making.

SQL operates on relational database management systems (RDBMS), where data is organized into structured tables. Each table contains rows (records) and columns (fields) to ensure a structured, predictable format.

Key Features:

• **Declarative Language:** You state *what* you want to do, and the database decides *how* to do it.

• **Standardized:** Although different systems have extensions, SQL's core commands (SELECT, INSERT, UPDATE, DELETE) are universally supported.

.

1.2 Importance of SQL in Modern Databases

SQL is foundational to modern data management. Here's why:

1. **Widespread Use:** Most database systems, including MySQL, PostgreSQL, Oracle, SQL Server, and SQLite, use SQL as their primary query language.

2. **Essential for Data Analysis:** SQL is a must-have skill for analyzing structured data in fields like business intelligence, data science, and software development.

3. Data Integrity and Accuracy: SQL enforces rules such as primary keys and foreign keys, ensuring data remains consistent and reliable.

4. Automation and Scalability: SQL queries can automate repetitive tasks and handle massive datasets efficiently.

5. Cross-Platform: SQL is platform-independent and integrates seamlessly with various programming languages like Python, Java, and C#.

Real-World Applications:

• Generating reports from sales or inventory systems.

• Querying customer data in e-commerce platforms.

• Aggregating and visualizing big data in analytics pipelines.

1.3 A Brief History of SQL

The origins of SQL date back to the 1970s, coinciding with the rise of relational databases.

1970: Edgar F. Codd published a paper introducing the concept of relational databases at IBM.

1974-1975: IBM researchers Donald D. Chamberlin and Raymond F. Boyce developed SEQUEL (Structured English Query Language), which later became SQL.

1979: Oracle released the first commercial implementation of SQL, revolutionizing the database industry.

1986: SQL became an ANSI (American National Standards Institute) standard.

1989: The ISO (International Organization for Standardization) adopted SQL as an international standard.

Present Day: SQL has evolved with extensions (e.g., PL/pgSQL for PostgreSQL, T-SQL for SQL Server) and supports modern needs like JSON and XML data manipulation.

1.4 Setting Up Your Environment

Before you start writing SQL, you need a database

management system (DBMS) and a client tool. Here are popular options:

1. Choosing a DBMS:

o **MySQL:** Open-source, widely used for web applications.

o **PostgreSQL:** Known for robustness, compliance with SQL standards, and advanced features like JSON support.

o **SQLite:** Lightweight, serverless, and great for small applications or embedded devices.

o **Microsoft SQL Server:** Enterprise-grade with integration into Microsoft ecosystems.

o **Oracle Database:** Common in large-scale enterprise environments.

2. Installing a DBMS:

o **MySQL:** Download from MySQL's official site.

o **PostgreSQL:** Download from PostgreSQL's official site.

o **SQLite:** Usually comes pre-installed on many systems; otherwise, download from SQLite's site.

3. Database Clients:

○ **Command Line Tools:** Most DBMSs include a built-in CLI for direct query execution.

○ **Graphical Tools:**

■ **MySQL Workbench:** A GUI for MySQL.

■ **pgAdmin:** A feature-rich tool for PostgreSQL.

■ **DBeaver:** A universal database management tool compatible with most DBMSs.

4. Setting Up:

○ Install your chosen DBMS.

○ Configure user accounts and passwords (e.g., set a root password in MySQL).

○ Create a sample database to practice.

1.5 SQL Syntax Basics

SQL syntax is simple and English-like. It is composed of various statements used to interact with data. Key components include:

1. Statements:

○ **SELECT:** Retrieves data from a table.

○ **INSERT:** Adds new records to a table.

○ **UPDATE:** Modifies existing data.

○ **DELETE:** Removes records from a table.

○ **CREATE TABLE:** Defines a new table.

2. Basic SQL Structure:

sql:

SELECT column1, column2

FROM table_name

WHERE condition

ORDER BY column1;

Example:

sql:

SELECT first_name, last_name

FROM employees

WHERE salary > 50000

ORDER BY last_name;

3. Keywords: Reserved words like SELECT, WHERE, and FROM are case-insensitive but usually written in uppercase for clarity.

4. Clauses:

○ WHERE: Filters data based on a condition.

○ ORDER BY: Sorts the result set.

○ GROUP BY: Aggregates data based on a column.

5. Best Practices:

○ Use proper indentation for readability.

○ End every statement with a semicolon (;).

○ Avoid using ambiguous column names in queries.

By mastering these foundational topics, you'll be ready to write efficient SQL queries and work with relational databases.

2

UNDERSTANDING DATABASES

2.1 What is a Database?

A **database** is an organized collection of data that can be easily accessed, managed, and updated. It allows users and applications to:

• **Store data:** Keep records of information systematically.

• **Retrieve data:** Query specific information when needed.

• **Update data:** Modify or add new records.

• **Delete data:** Remove outdated or unnecessary information.

Databases are designed to handle large volumes of data efficiently, ensuring accuracy and availability. They are widely used in applications ranging from small websites to enterprise-level systems.

2.2 Types of Databases (Relational vs. Non-relational)

1. Relational Databases:

○ **Definition:** Organize data into tables with rows and columns, following a structured schema.

○ **Examples:** MySQL, PostgreSQL, SQLite, SQL Server, Oracle Database.

○ **Key Features:**

■ Uses SQL for querying.

■ Data is linked using relationships (e.g., foreign keys).

■ Ensures data integrity through constraints.

2. Non-relational Databases (NoSQL):

○ **Definition:** Do not rely on a tabular schema.

Designed for unstructured or semi-structured data.

○ **Examples:** MongoDB (document-based), Cassandra (columnar), Redis (key-value), Neo4j (graph-based).

○ **Key Features:**

■ Flexible schema design.

■ Scales horizontally for large datasets.

■ Commonly used in real-time applications like social media, IoT, and analytics.

Comparison:

Feature	Relational Databases	Non-relational Databases
Structure	Fixed schema, tables, rows	Flexible schema, various models
Scalability	Vertical (add resources)	Horizontal (add nodes)
Query Language	SQL	No standard query language
Use Case	Structured, transactional data	Unstructured, large-scale data

2.3 Tables, Rows, and Columns Explained

1. Table:

○ A table is the primary structure in a relational database.

○ Example:

EmployeeID	FirstName	LastName	Department

2. Row:

○ A single record in a table.

○ Example: | 101 | John | Doe | HR |

3. Column:

○ A field in a table that contains a specific type of data.

○ Example:

• EmployeeID: Integer

• FirstName: String

Conceptual Breakdown:

• Tables = Spreadsheet.

• Rows = Individual entries in the spreadsheet.

• Columns = Headings of the spreadsheet defining the type of data.

.   .   .

2.4 Primary Keys and Foreign Keys

I. Primary Key:

○ A unique identifier for each row in a table.

○ **Purpose:** Ensures no duplicate records.

○ **Characteristics:**

▪ Unique across the table.

▪ Cannot be NULL.

○ **Example:**

EmployeeID (Primary Key)	FirstName	LastName
101	John	Doe

2. Foreign Key:

○ A column that creates a relationship between two tables.

○ **Purpose:** Ensures referential integrity.

○ **Example:**

▪ Orders table references the Customers table.

CustomerID (Primary Key)	Name
1	Alice
2	Bob

OrderID	CustomerID (Foreign Key)	Amount
201	1	$100

2.5 Relational Database Management Systems (RDBMS)

An **RDBMS** is software that manages relational databases. It enables users to interact with data through SQL and ensures data consistency and security.

Key Features:

1. Data Storage and Retrieval: Stores data in structured tables and provides efficient querying.

2. Data Integrity: Maintains consistency through constraints like primary keys and foreign keys.

3. Concurrency Control: Supports multiple users accessing the database simultaneously.

4. Backup and Recovery: Ensures data is recoverable in case of failure.

5. Scalability: Handles growing amounts of data and users.

Popular RDBMS Software:

• **MySQL:** Free, open-source, commonly used in web development.

• **PostgreSQL:** Advanced features with robust standards compliance.

• **Oracle Database:** Enterprise-grade with extensive security and scalability.

• **Microsoft SQL Server:** Deep integration with Microsoft tools.

• **SQLite:** Lightweight, serverless option for small applications.

GETTING STARTED WITH SQL QUERIES

3.1 Writing Your First SQL Query

A SQL query is a command written in SQL to interact with a database. Let's start with the most basic query to retrieve data.

Example Database Table (Employees):

EmployeeID	FirstName	LastName	Department	Salary
1	John	Doe	HR	50000
2	Jane	Smith	IT	60000
3	Alice	Brown	Finance	55000

Your First Query:

Sql:

SELECT * FROM Employees;

- **Explanation:**

○ SELECT retrieves data.

○ * indicates all columns.

○ FROM Employees specifies the table to query.

Output:

EmployeeID	FirstName	LastName	Department	Salary
1	John	Doe	HR	50000
2	Jane	Smith	IT	60000
3	Alice	Brown	Finance	55000

3.2 SELECT Statement Basics

The SELECT statement is the foundation of SQL querying, used to fetch specific data from a table.

Basic Syntax:

Sql:

SELECT column1, column2

FROM table_name;

Example:

Retrieve only the FirstName and Department from the Employees table:

Sql:

SELECT FirstName, Department

FROM Employees;

Output:

FirstName	Department
John	HR
Jane	IT
Alice	Finance

Aliases:

To rename columns for clarity, use the AS keyword:

Sql:

SELECT FirstName AS Name, Department AS Dept

FROM Employees;

Output:

Name	Dept
John	HR
Jane	IT
Alice	Finance

3.3 Filtering Data with WHERE

The WHERE clause filters rows based on a condition.

Syntax:

Sql:

SELECT column1, column2

FROM table_name

WHERE condition;

Example:

Retrieve employees in the IT department:

Sql:

SELECT FirstName, Department

FROM Employees

WHERE Department = 'IT';

Output:

FirstName	Department
Jane	IT

Using Comparison Operators:

- =: Equal to.

- < / >: Less than / Greater than.

- <= / >=: Less than or equal / Greater than or equal.

- != or <>: Not equal.

Example: Find employees with a salary greater than 55000:

Sql:

SELECT FirstName, Salary

FROM Employees

WHERE Salary > 55000;

Output:

FirstName	Salary
Jane	60000

3.4 Sorting Data with ORDER BY

The ORDER BY clause sorts query results.

Syntax:

Sql:

SELECT column1, column2

FROM table_name

ORDER BY column1 [ASC | DESC];

Example:

Sort employees by salary in ascending order:

Sql:

SELECT FirstName, Salary

FROM Employees

ORDER BY Salary ASC;

Output:

FirstName	Salary
John	50000
Alice	55000
Jane	60000

Sort employees by salary in descending order:

Sql:

SELECT FirstName, Salary

FROM Employees

ORDER BY Salary DESC;

Output:

FirstName	Salary
Jane	60000
Alice	55000
John	50000

3.5 Limiting Results with LIMIT

The LIMIT clause restricts the number of rows returned.

Syntax:

Sql:

SELECT column1, column2

FROM table_name

LIMIT number;

Example:

Retrieve only the first two rows:

Sql:

SELECT FirstName, Salary

FROM Employees

LIMIT 2;

Output:

FirstName	Salary
John	50000
Jane	60000

Using OFFSET:

Combine LIMIT with OFFSET to skip rows:

Sql:

SELECT FirstName, Salary

FROM Employees

LIMIT 1 OFFSET 1;

- **Explanation:** Skip the first row, return the next row.

Output:

FirstName	Salary
Jane	60000

4

WORKING WITH DATA

4.1 Inserting Data: INSERT INTO

The INSERT INTO statement adds new records to a table.

Syntax:

Sql:

INSERT INTO table_name (column1, column2, column3)

VALUES (value1, value2, value3);

Example:

Add a new employee to the Employees table:

Sql:

INSERT INTO Employees (EmployeeID, First-Name, LastName, Department, Salary)

VALUES (4, 'Mark', 'Taylor', 'Marketing', 48000);

Result:

EmployeeID	FirstName	LastName	Department	Salary
1	John	Doe	HR	50000
2	Jane	Smith	IT	60000
3	Alice	Brown	Finance	55000
4	Mark	Taylor	Marketing	48000

Inserting Without Specifying Columns:

If you are inserting values for all columns in the correct order, column names can be omitted:

Sql:

INSERT INTO Employees

VALUES (5, 'Linda', 'Green', 'Sales', 52000);

4.2 Updating Data: UPDATE

The UPDATE statement modifies existing data in a table.

Syntax:

Sql:

UPDATE table_name

SET columnI = valueI, column2 = value2

WHERE condition;

Example:

Update the salary of the employee with EmployeeID = 3:

Sql:

UPDATE Employees

SET Salary = 58000

WHERE EmployeeID = 3;

Result:

EmployeeID	FirstName	LastName	Department	Salary
3	Alice	Brown	Finance	58000

Warning:

• **Always use a WHERE clause** to avoid updating all rows accidentally.

. . .

4.3 Deleting Data: DELETE

The DELETE statement removes records from a table.

Syntax:

Sql:

DELETE FROM table_name

WHERE condition;

Example:

Remove the employee with EmployeeID = 4:

Sql:

DELETE FROM Employees

WHERE EmployeeID = 4;

Result:

EmployeeID	FirstName	LastName	Department	Salary
1	John	Doe	HR	50000
2	Jane	Smith	IT	60000
3	Alice	Brown	Finance	58000

Deleting All Rows: To remove all rows but keep the table structure:

Sql:

DELETE FROM Employees;

4.4 Handling NULL Values

NULL represents missing or unknown data in a database.

Key Points:

• NULL is not the same as zero or an empty string.

• Special operators are required to work with NULL values.

Checking for NULL: Use IS NULL or IS NOT NULL:

Sql:

SELECT FirstName

FROM Employees

WHERE Salary IS NULL;

Replacing NULL: Use the COALESCE function to replace NULL with a default value:

Sql:

SELECT FirstName, COALESCE(Salary, 0) AS AdjustedSalary

FROM Employees;

Inserting NULL: You can explicitly insert NULL into a column:

Sql:

INSERT INTO Employees (EmployeeID, First-Name, LastName, Department, Salary)

VALUES (6, 'Emma', 'White', 'IT', NULL);

4.5 Best Practices for Data Integrity

Maintaining data integrity ensures the accuracy and consistency of data.

1. Define Constraints:

• **NOT NULL:** Ensures a column cannot have NULL values.

• **UNIQUE:** Prevents duplicate values in a column.

• **CHECK:** Validates data based on a condition.

- **DEFAULT:** Provides a default value if none is specified.

Example:

Sql:

CREATE TABLE Employees (

EmployeeID INT PRIMARY KEY,

FirstName VARCHAR(50) NOT NULL,

LastName VARCHAR(50),

Department VARCHAR(50),

Salary DECIMAL(10, 2) CHECK (Salary > 0)

);

2. Use Transactions: Group related operations into a single transaction to ensure atomicity:

Sql:

BEGIN TRANSACTION;

UPDATE Employees SET Salary = Salary + 1000 WHERE Department = 'IT';

DELETE FROM Employees WHERE EmployeeID = 10;

COMMIT;

3. Normalize Your Database: Organize data to reduce redundancy and dependency. Use foreign keys to maintain relationships between tables.

4. Regularly Backup Data: Schedule backups to protect against data loss.

5. Validate Input: Implement input validation to prevent SQL injection and maintain clean data.

ADVANCED QUERYING

5.1 Aggregate Functions: COUNT, SUM, AVG, MIN, MAX

Aggregate functions perform calculations on a set of rows and return a single result.

COUNT:

Returns the number of rows.

SUM:

Calculates the total of a column.

AVG:

Computes the average value.

MIN:

Finds the smallest value.

MAX:

Finds the largest value.

Example Table (Sales):

SaleID	Product	Quantity	Price
1	Laptop	2	1000
2	Mouse	5	20
3	Keyboard	3	50

Examples:

1. COUNT: Count the number of sales:

Sql:

SELECT COUNT(*) AS TotalSales FROM Sales;

Result: 3

2. SUM: Calculate total revenue:

Sql:

SELECT SUM(Quantity * Price) AS TotalRevenue FROM Sales;

Result: 2150

3. AVG: Find the average price of products:

Sql:

SELECT AVG(Price) AS AveragePrice FROM Sales;

Result: 356.67

4. MIN / MAX: Find the cheapest and most expensive products:

Sql:

SELECT MIN(Price) AS MinPrice, MAX(Price) AS MaxPrice FROM Sales;

Result: MinPrice: 20, MaxPrice: 1000

5.2 GROUP BY and HAVING Clauses

The GROUP BY clause groups rows that have the same values in specified columns. The HAVING clause filters grouped results.

Syntax:

Sql:

SELECT column1, aggregate_function(column2)

FROM table_name

GROUP BY column1

HAVING condition;

Example Table (Orders):

OrderID	Customer	Quantity
1	Alice	3
2	Bob	2
3	Alice	5
4	Bob	4

Examples:

1. GROUP BY: Find total quantity ordered by each customer:

Sql:

SELECT Customer, SUM(Quantity) AS TotalQuantity

FROM Orders

GROUP BY Customer;

Result:

Customer	TotalQuantity
Alice	8
Bob	6

2. HAVING: Show only customers with total quantities greater than 5:

Sql:

SELECT Customer, SUM(Quantity) AS Total-Quantity

FROM Orders

GROUP BY Customer

HAVING SUM(Quantity) > 5;

Result:

Customer	TotalQuantity
Alice	8

5.3 Combining Results with UNION and UNION ALL

The UNION operator combines the results of two or more SELECT statements, removing duplicates. UNION ALL retains duplicates.

Syntax:

Sql:

SELECT column1, column2 FROM table1

UNION

SELECT column1, column2 FROM table2;

Examples:

Combine two product lists:

Sql:

SELECT Product FROM Sales

UNION

SELECT Product FROM NewArrivals;

Retain duplicates:

Sql:

SELECT Product FROM Sales

UNION ALL

SELECT Product FROM NewArrivals;

5.4 Subqueries: What, Why, and How

A **subquery** is a query nested inside another

query. Subqueries are often used to filter data dynamically.

Syntax:

Sql:

SELECT column1

FROM table1

WHERE column2 = (SELECT column FROM table2 WHERE condition);

Example Table (Employees):

EmployeeID	Name	Department	Salary
1	John	IT	60000
2	Alice	HR	50000
3	Bob	IT	70000

Example:

Find employees earning more than the average salary:

Sql:

SELECT Name

FROM Employees

WHERE Salary > (SELECT AVG(Salary) FROM Employees);

Result:

Name
Bob

5.5 Working with Joins (INNER, LEFT, RIGHT, FULL OUTER)

Joins combine rows from two or more tables based on a related column.

INNER JOIN: Returns only matching rows.

LEFT JOIN: Returns all rows from the left table, with matching rows from the right.

RIGHT JOIN: Returns all rows from the right table, with matching rows from the left.

FULL OUTER JOIN: Returns all rows, with NULL for non-matching rows.

Example Tables:

Employees Table:

EmployeeID	Name	Department
1	John	IT
2	Alice	HR

Departments Table:

DepartmentID	Department
1	IT
2	HR
3	Marketing

Examples:

1. INNER JOIN:

Sql:

SELECT Employees.Name, Departments.Department

FROM Employees

INNER JOIN Departments ON Employees.Department = Departments.Department;

2. LEFT JOIN:

Sql:

SELECT Employees.Name, Departments.Department

FROM Employees

LEFT JOIN Departments ON Employees.Department = Departments.Department;

3. FULL OUTER JOIN:

Sql:

SELECT   Employees.Name,   Departments.Department

FROM Employees

FULL OUTER JOIN Departments ON Employees.Department = Departments.Department;

CREATING AND MANAGING TABLES

6.1 Creating Tables: CREATE TABLE

The CREATE TABLE statement is used to define the structure of a table, including its columns, data types, and constraints.

Syntax:

Sql:

CREATE TABLE table_name (

column1 datatype constraint,

column2 datatype constraint,

...

);

Example: Create an Employees table:

Sql:

CREATE TABLE Employees (

EmployeeID INT PRIMARY KEY,

FirstName VARCHAR(50) NOT NULL,

LastName VARCHAR(50),

Department VARCHAR(50),

Salary DECIMAL(10, 2) CHECK (Salary > 0)

);

Explanation:

• EmployeeID: Integer, primary key.

• FirstName: Variable-length string, cannot be NULL.

• Salary: Decimal with a check constraint ensuring positive values.

6.2 Modifying Tables: ALTER TABLE

The ALTER TABLE statement is used to make changes to an existing table, such as adding, deleting, or modifying columns.

Syntax:

• **Add a column:**

Sql:

ALTER TABLE table_name

ADD column_name datatype;

• **Modify a column:**

Sql:

ALTER TABLE table_name

MODIFY column_name datatype;

• **Delete a column:**

Sql:

ALTER TABLE table_name

DROP COLUMN column_name;

. . .

Examples:

1. Add a column for HireDate:

Sql:

ALTER TABLE Employees

ADD HireDate DATE;

2. Modify the Department column to allow 100 characters:

Sql:

ALTER TABLE Employees

MODIFY Department VARCHAR(100);

3. Remove the HireDate column:

Sql:

ALTER TABLE Employees

DROP COLUMN HireDate;

. . .

6.3 Deleting Tables: DROP TABLE

The DROP TABLE statement permanently removes a table and its data.

Syntax:

Sql:

DROP TABLE table_name;

Example: Delete the Employees table:

Sql:

DROP TABLE Employees;

Warning: This action cannot be undone. Ensure you have backups before dropping a table.

6.4 Understanding Data Types

Data types define the type of data a column can hold. Common data types include:

Numeric

INT, DECIMAL: Whole numbers, precise decimals.

String/Text

VARCHAR, TEXT: Variable-length strings, longer text data.

Date/Time

DATE, DATETIME: Dates, timestamps.

Boolean

BOOLEAN: True or false values.

Binary

BLOB: Binary large objects (e.g., images, files).

Examples:

1. Define a numeric column:

Sql:

Salary DECIMAL(10, 2);

○ 10: Total digits.

○ 2: Digits after the decimal point.

2. Define a string column:

Sql:

FirstName VARCHAR(50);

○ 50: Maximum length of the string.

6.5 Constraints: NOT NULL, UNIQUE, CHECK, DEFAULT

Constraints ensure data integrity by enforcing rules on columns.

1. NOT NULL:

Ensures a column cannot have NULL values.

Sql:

FirstName VARCHAR(50) NOT NULL;

2. UNIQUE:

Ensures all values in a column are unique.

Sql:

Email VARCHAR(100) UNIQUE;

3. CHECK:

Enforces a condition on values.

Sql:

Salary DECIMAL(10, 2) CHECK (Salary > 0);

4. DEFAULT:

Provides a default value if none is specified.

Sql:

Department VARCHAR(50) DEFAULT 'General';

5. Primary Key (PK):

Uniquely identifies each row in the table.

Sql:

EmployeeID INT PRIMARY KEY;

6. Foreign Key (FK):

Links data between two tables.

Sql:

FOREIGN KEY (DepartmentID) REFERENCES Departments(DepartmentID);

Example with Multiple Constraints:

Sql:

```
CREATE TABLE Employees (

EmployeeID INT PRIMARY KEY,

FirstName VARCHAR(50) NOT NULL,

Email VARCHAR(100) UNIQUE,

Salary DECIMAL(10, 2) CHECK (Salary > 0),

Department VARCHAR(50) DEFAULT 'General'

);
```

INDEXES AND PERFORMANCE OPTIMIZATION

7.1 What are Indexes?

An **index** is a database object that improves the speed of data retrieval operations. It acts like a "lookup table" to locate data quickly without scanning the entire table.

• **Analogy:** Think of an index in a book—it helps you find topics without reading every page.

• **Structure:** Most databases use a B-tree or hash-based structure for indexes.

• **Types of Indexes:**

○ **Clustered Index:** Rearranges the physical order of the data to match the index.

o **Non-clustered Index:** Creates a separate structure to point to the original table data.

7.2 Creating and Using Indexes

Indexes are created on one or more columns to speed up queries.

Syntax:

Sql:

CREATE INDEX index_name

ON table_name (column1, column2, ...);

Examples:

1. Create an index on the LastName column:

Sql:

CREATE INDEX idx_lastname

ON Employees (LastName);

2. Create a composite index on LastName and FirstName:

Sql:

CREATE INDEX idx_name

ON Employees (LastName, FirstName);

Dropping an Index: If an index is no longer needed, you can remove it:

Sql:

DROP INDEX index_name ON table_name;

7.3 How Indexes Improve Query Performance

Indexes optimize query performance by reducing the number of rows scanned.

Without Index:

• A query like SELECT * FROM Employees WHERE LastName = 'Smith'; requires a **full table scan**, checking every row.

With Index:

• The database uses the index to locate matching rows directly, significantly speeding up the query.

Trade-offs:

• **Advantages:**

○ Faster SELECT queries.

○ Efficient filtering, sorting, and joins.

• **Disadvantages:**

○ Slower INSERT, UPDATE, DELETE operations (as indexes need updating).

○ Increased storage requirements.

7.4 Understanding Query Execution Plans

A **query execution plan** shows how the database executes a query. It helps identify bottlenecks and optimize performance.

Generating Execution Plans:

1. MySQL:

Sql:

EXPLAIN SELECT * FROM Employees WHERE LastName = 'Smith';

· · ·

2. PostgreSQL:

Sql:

EXPLAIN ANALYZE SELECT * FROM Employees WHERE LastName = 'Smith';

Key Components:

• **Table Scan:** Indicates a full scan of the table (inefficient for large datasets).

• **Index Scan:** Indicates that an index was used (efficient).

• **Join Type:** Shows how tables are joined (e.g., nested loop, hash join).

Example Output:

Step	Rows	Cost
Index Scan (idx_lastname)	10	0.5

7.5 Common Optimization Techniques

1. Optimize Index Usage:

○ Create indexes on columns frequently used in WHERE, JOIN, GROUP BY, and ORDER BY clauses.

○ Avoid over-indexing, which increases storage and slows write operations.

2. Use Appropriate Data Types:

○ Choose the smallest data type that fits your data (e.g., INT vs. BIGINT).

3. *Avoid SELECT :*

○ Fetch only the required columns to reduce data transfer and processing.

Inefficient:

Sql:

SELECT * FROM Employees;

Efficient:

Sql:

SELECT FirstName, LastName FROM Employees;

4. Partitioning and Sharding:

○ **Partitioning:** Divides a table into smaller parts based on a column (e.g., date).

○ **Sharding:** Distributes data across multiple servers.

5. Use Caching:

○ Cache frequently accessed results in memory to avoid repeated computations.

6. Optimize JOINs:

○ Ensure indexed columns are used in JOIN conditions.

○ Use INNER JOINs when possible, as they are faster than OUTER JOINs.

7. Analyze Query Performance Regularly:

○ Use tools like EXPLAIN or database monitoring tools to detect slow queries and refine them.

WORKING WITH RELATIONSHIPS

8.1 Understanding One-to-One, One-to-Many, and Many-to-Many Relationships

Relational databases use relationships to connect tables. These relationships define how data in one table relates to data in another.

1. One-to-One Relationship:

○ Each row in Table A is linked to only one row in Table B and vice versa.

○ **Example:** A Users table and a Profiles table (each user has exactly one profile).

○ **Implementation:** Use a primary key in one table and a unique foreign key in the other.

Example Schema:

Sql:

CREATE TABLE Users (

UserID INT PRIMARY KEY,

UserName VARCHAR(50)

);

CREATE TABLE Profiles (

ProfileID INT PRIMARY KEY,

UserID INT UNIQUE,

Bio TEXT,

FOREIGN   KEY   (UserID)   REFERENCES Users(UserID)

);

2. One-to-Many Relationship:

○ A row in Table A can have multiple related rows in Table B, but a row in Table B is related to only one row in Table A.

○ **Example:** A Categories table and a Products table (each category can have many products).

○ **Implementation:** Use a foreign key in the child table (Table B).

Example Schema:

Sql:

CREATE TABLE Categories (

CategoryID INT PRIMARY KEY,

CategoryName VARCHAR(50)

);

CREATE TABLE Products (

ProductID INT PRIMARY KEY,

ProductName VARCHAR(50),

CategoryID INT,

FOREIGN KEY (CategoryID) REFERENCES Categories(CategoryID)

);

· · ·

3. Many-to-Many Relationship:

○ Rows in Table A can relate to multiple rows in Table B, and rows in Table B can relate to multiple rows in Table A.

○ **Example:** A Students table and a Courses table (students can enroll in multiple courses, and courses can have multiple students).

○ **Implementation:** Use a junction table to handle the relationship.

Example Schema:

Sql:

CREATE TABLE Students (

StudentID INT PRIMARY KEY,

StudentName VARCHAR(50)

);

CREATE TABLE Courses (

CourseID INT PRIMARY KEY,

CourseName VARCHAR(50)

);

```
CREATE TABLE Enrollments (

StudentID INT,

CourseID INT,

PRIMARY KEY (StudentID, CourseID),

FOREIGN KEY (StudentID) REFERENCES Students(StudentID),

FOREIGN KEY (CourseID) REFERENCES Courses(CourseID)

);
```

8.2 Using Foreign Keys to Define Relationships

A **foreign key** is a column in one table that references the primary key in another table. It enforces the relationship between the two tables.

Benefits of Foreign Keys:

• Maintains data integrity by ensuring only valid values exist in the related table.

• Prevents orphaned rows (e.g., a product with a non-existent category).

Syntax:

Sql:

CREATE TABLE ChildTable (

Column1 INT,

Column2 INT,

FOREIGN KEY (Column1) REFERENCES Parent-Table(PrimaryKeyColumn)

);

Example: Link a Products table to a Categories table:

Sql:

CREATE TABLE Categories (

CategoryID INT PRIMARY KEY,

CategoryName VARCHAR(50)

);

CREATE TABLE Products (

ProductID INT PRIMARY KEY,

ProductName VARCHAR(50),

CategoryID INT,

FOREIGN KEY (CategoryID) REFERENCES Categories(CategoryID)

);

8.3 Referential Integrity and Cascading Actions

Referential Integrity:

- Ensures that relationships between tables remain consistent.

Example: A Products table cannot reference a CategoryID that doesn't exist in the Categories table.

Cascading Actions: Cascading actions define what happens to related rows in child tables when a row in the parent table is updated or deleted.

1. ON DELETE CASCADE:

○ Deletes child rows automatically when the parent row is deleted.

Sql:

FOREIGN KEY (CategoryID) REFERENCES Categories(CategoryID) ON DELETE CASCADE;

2. ON UPDATE CASCADE:

○ Updates the foreign key value in child rows when the parent key is updated.

Sql:

FOREIGN KEY (CategoryID) REFERENCES Categories(CategoryID) ON UPDATE CASCADE;

3. SET NULL:

○ Sets the foreign key value to NULL in the child rows when the parent row is deleted or updated.

Sql:

FOREIGN KEY (CategoryID) REFERENCES Categories(CategoryID) ON DELETE SET NULL;

4. NO ACTION/RESTRICT:

○ Prevents the deletion or update of a parent row if related child rows exist.

Sql:

FOREIGN KEY (CategoryID) REFERENCES Categories(CategoryID) ON DELETE NO ACTION;

Example with Cascades:

Sql:

CREATE TABLE Categories (

CategoryID INT PRIMARY KEY,

CategoryName VARCHAR(50)

);

CREATE TABLE Products (

ProductID INT PRIMARY KEY,

ProductName VARCHAR(50),

CategoryID INT,

FOREIGN KEY (CategoryID) REFERENCES Categories(CategoryID)

ON DELETE CASCADE

ON UPDATE CASCADE

);

9

SQL FUNCTIONS AND EXPRESSIONS

9.1 String Functions (CONCAT, LENGTH, SUBSTRING)

1. CONCAT:

Combines two or more strings into one.

Syntax:

Sql:

CONCAT(string1, string2, ...)

Example:

Sql:

SELECT CONCAT('Hello', ' ', 'World') AS Greeting;

. . .

Result: Hello World

2. LENGTH:

Returns the number of characters in a string (in bytes).

Syntax:

Sql:

LENGTH(string)

Example:

Sql:

SELECT   LENGTH('SQL   Functions')   AS
StringLength;

Result: 13

3. SUBSTRING:

Extracts a portion of a string.

Syntax:

Sql:

SUBSTRING(string, start_position, length)

Example:

Sql:

SELECT SUBSTRING('Database Management', 1, 8) AS ExtractedPart;

Result: Database

9.2 Date and Time Functions (NOW, DATE_ADD, DATE_FORMAT)

1. NOW:

Returns the current date and time.

Syntax:

Sql:

NOW()

Example:

Sql:

SELECT NOW() AS CurrentDateTime;

Result: 2024-12-15 10:00:00

2. DATE_ADD:

Adds a specified interval to a date.

Syntax:

Sql:

DATE_ADD(date, INTERVAL value unit)

Example:

Sql:

SELECT DATE_ADD('2024-12-15', INTERVAL 7 DAY) AS OneWeekLater;

Result: 2024-12-22

3. DATE_FORMAT:

Formats a date value according to a specified format.

Syntax:

Sql:

DATE_FORMAT(date, format)

Example:

Sql:

SELECT DATE_FORMAT(NOW(), '%Y-%m-%d %H:%i:%s') AS FormattedDateTime;

Result: 2024-12-15 10:00:00

9.3 Mathematical Functions (ROUND, ABS, CEIL)

1. ROUND:

Rounds a number to the specified number of decimal places.

Syntax:

Sql:

ROUND(number, decimal_places)

Example:

Sql:

SELECT ROUND(123.456, 2) AS RoundedNumber;

Result: 123.46

2. ABS:

Returns the absolute value of a number.

Syntax:

Sql:

ABS(number)

Example:

Sql:

SELECT ABS(-25) AS AbsoluteValue;

Result: 25

.   .   .

3. CEIL:

Rounds a number up to the nearest integer.

Syntax:

Sql:

CEIL(number)

Example:

Sql:

SELECT CEIL(4.2) AS CeilingValue;

Result: 5

9.4 Conditional Statements (CASE, IF, COALESCE)

1. CASE:

Allows conditional logic in SQL queries.

Syntax:

Sql:

CASE

WHEN condition THEN result

[WHEN condition THEN result ...]

[ELSE result]

END

Example:

Sql:

SELECT

ProductName,

CASE

WHEN Price > 100 THEN 'Expensive'

ELSE 'Affordable'

END AS PriceCategory

FROM Products;

2. IF:

Returns a value based on a condition.

Syntax:

Sql:

IF(condition, true_result, false_result)

Example:

Sql:

SELECT IF(Salary > 50000, 'High', 'Low') AS SalaryCategory FROM Employees;

3. COALESCE:

Returns the first non-NULL value in a list.

Syntax:

Sql:

COALESCE(value1, value2, ...)

Example:

Sql:

SELECT COALESCE(NULL, NULL, 'FallbackValue') AS Result;

Result: FallbackValue

TRANSACTIONS AND ERROR HANDLING

10.1 What are Transactions?

A **transaction** is a sequence of SQL operations that are executed as a single unit of work. Transactions ensure **ACID** properties to maintain data integrity:

- **Atomicity:** All operations are executed, or none are.

- **Consistency:** The database remains in a valid state before and after the transaction.

- **Isolation:** Transactions do not interfere with each other.

- **Durability:** Once a transaction is committed, changes are permanent.

Example Use Cases:

- Transferring money between bank accounts.

- Placing an order in an e-commerce system.

- Updating inventory after a purchase.

Syntax:

Sql:

START TRANSACTION;

-- SQL operations here

COMMIT; -- Save changes

10.2 COMMIT and ROLLBACK Explained

1. COMMIT:

○ Saves all changes made during the transaction to the database.

○ Once committed, the changes are permanent and visible to other users.

Example:

Sql:

START TRANSACTION;

UPDATE Accounts SET Balance = Balance - 100
WHERE AccountID = 1;

UPDATE Accounts SET Balance = Balance + 100
WHERE AccountID = 2;

COMMIT;

2. ROLLBACK:

○ Undoes all changes made during the transaction, returning the database to its state before the transaction started.

Example:

Sql:

START TRANSACTION;

UPDATE Accounts SET Balance = Balance - 100
WHERE AccountID = 1;

-- Error occurs here

ROLLBACK;

Important Notes:

• If no COMMIT or ROLLBACK is issued, changes remain in a pending state.

• Use transactions for critical operations where partial updates could corrupt data.

10.3 Ensuring Atomicity with Transactions

Atomicity ensures that all parts of a transaction succeed or none do. SQL transactions achieve atomicity by using COMMIT and ROLLBACK.

Example Scenario: Transferring money between two accounts:

Sql:

START TRANSACTION;

UPDATE Accounts SET Balance = Balance - 100 WHERE AccountID = 1;

UPDATE Accounts SET Balance = Balance + 100 WHERE AccountID = 2;

IF (ERROR) THEN

ROLLBACK;

ELSE

COMMIT;

END IF;

Key Points:

• Errors during the transaction trigger a rollback to maintain data consistency.

• Atomicity prevents partial updates.

10.4 Error Handling in SQL

Error handling ensures that unexpected issues during SQL operations are managed gracefully.

1. TRY-CATCH Blocks (Supported in some RDBMS, like SQL Server):

○   Captures errors and allows custom error handling.

Example (SQL Server):

Sql:

```
BEGIN TRY

BEGIN TRANSACTION;

UPDATE Accounts SET Balance = Balance - 100
WHERE AccountID = 1;

UPDATE Accounts SET Balance = Balance + 100
WHERE AccountID = 2;

COMMIT;

END TRY

BEGIN CATCH

ROLLBACK;

PRINT ERROR_MESSAGE();

END CATCH;
```

2. Error Codes (MySQL Example):

Use error codes or conditions to handle issues.

Sql:

```
START TRANSACTION;
```

UPDATE Accounts SET Balance = Balance - 100 WHERE AccountID = 1;

IF (ROW_COUNT() = 0) THEN

ROLLBACK;

SIGNAL SQLSTATE '45000' SET MESSAGE_TEXT = 'Transaction failed.';

END IF;

COMMIT;

3. SAVEPOINTS:

Allows partial rollback within a transaction.

Example:

Sql:

START TRANSACTION;

SAVEPOINT Savepoint1;

UPDATE Accounts SET Balance = Balance - 100 WHERE AccountID = 1;

ROLLBACK TO Savepoint1; -- Undo only changes after Savepoint1

COMMIT;

4. Validation and Logging:

○   Validate inputs before executing queries to prevent errors.

○ Log errors to a separate table for debugging.

WORKING WITH VIEWS

11.1 Creating Views: CREATE VIEW

A **view** is a virtual table created from the result of a SQL query. It does not store data itself but dynamically displays data from the underlying tables.

Syntax:

Sql:

CREATE VIEW view_name AS

SELECT column1, column2

FROM table_name

WHERE condition;

Example: Create a view to display high-salary employees:

Sql:

CREATE VIEW HighSalaryEmployees AS

SELECT EmployeeID, FirstName, LastName, Salary

FROM Employees

WHERE Salary > 50000;

Usage: Query the view like a regular table:

Sql:

SELECT * FROM HighSalaryEmployees;

11.2 Updating and Dropping Views

1. Updating a View:

To modify the definition of a view, use the CREATE OR REPLACE VIEW statement.

Sql:

CREATE OR REPLACE VIEW HighSalaryEm-ployees AS

SELECT EmployeeID, FirstName, LastName, Salary, Department

FROM Employees

WHERE Salary > 50000;

2. Dropping a View:

To remove a view, use the DROP VIEW statement.

Sql:

DROP VIEW view_name;

Example:

Sql:

DROP VIEW HighSalaryEmployees;

Note: Dropping a view does not affect the underlying tables.

11.3 Benefits of Using Views

1. Simplifies Complex Queries:

○ Encapsulates complex SQL logic into a reusable virtual table.

○ <u>Example:</u> Instead of writing a multi-join query repeatedly, define it as a view.

2. Enhances Security:

○ Restricts access to specific columns or rows in a table by exposing only what is defined in the view.

○ <u>Example:</u> A view can hide sensitive columns like SSN or Password.

3. Improves Data Consistency:

○ Ensures that users always see consistent data if the view logic centralizes business rules.

4. Abstracts Schema Changes:

○ Allows changes to the underlying table schema without affecting users accessing data through the view.

5. Readability:

○ Makes query results more readable with meaningful names and formatting.

. . .

11.4 Common Use Cases for Views

1. Simplifying Reports:

Combine multiple tables and columns into a single, easy-to-read format.

Sql:

CREATE VIEW SalesReport AS

SELECT Products.ProductName, SUM(Orders.Quantity) AS TotalQuantity

FROM Orders

INNER JOIN Products ON Orders.ProductID = Products.ProductID

GROUP BY Products.ProductName;

2. Restricting Data Access:

Limit user access to certain rows or columns.

Sql:

CREATE VIEW PublicEmployees AS

SELECT FirstName, LastName, Department

FROM Employees;

3. Reusable Query Logic:

Avoid rewriting the same complex queries by encapsulating them in views.

4. Data Transformation:

Pre-format data for better usability, such as date formats or calculated fields.

Sql:

CREATE VIEW FormattedDates AS

SELECT EmployeeID, DATE_FORMAT(HireDate, '%Y-%m-%d') AS HireDate

FROM Employees;

5. Debugging and Development:

Test and visualize intermediate query results while developing complex queries.

ADVANCED TOPICS

12.1 Stored Procedures and Functions

Stored Procedures:

• A stored procedure is a precompiled set of SQL statements stored in the database, which can be executed repeatedly.

• **Use Case:** Automating repetitive tasks or complex business logic.

Syntax for Creating a Stored Procedure:

Sql:

CREATE   PROCEDURE   procedure_name (parameters)

BEGIN

SQL statements;

END;

Example:

A procedure to increase salaries in a department:

Sql:

CREATE PROCEDURE IncreaseSalary(dept_-name VARCHAR(50), increment DECIMAL(10, 2))

BEGIN

UPDATE Employees

SET Salary = Salary + increment

WHERE Department = dept_name;

END;

Calling a Stored Procedure:

Sql:

CALL IncreaseSalary('HR', 5000);

Functions:

- Functions are similar to procedures but **must return a value and can be used in queries.**

Syntax for Creating a Function:

Sql:

CREATE FUNCTION function_name (parameters)

RETURNS datatype

BEGIN

RETURN expression;

END;

Example:

A function to calculate annual salary:

Sql:

CREATE FUNCTION AnnualSalary(monthly_salary DECIMAL(10, 2))

RETURNS DECIMAL(10, 2)

BEGIN

RETURN monthly_salary * 12;

END;

Usage:

Sql:

SELECT AnnualSalary(Salary) AS Annual FROM Employees;

12.2 Triggers and Their Use Cases

Triggers:

• A trigger is an automated action executed in response to an event (INSERT, UPDATE, DELETE) on a table.

Syntax for Creating a Trigger:

Sql:

CREATE TRIGGER trigger_name

AFTER | BEFORE event

ON table_name

FOR EACH ROW

BEGIN

SQL statements;

END;

Example:

Log changes to an Employees table:

Sql:

CREATE TRIGGER LogSalaryUpdate

AFTER UPDATE ON Employees

FOR EACH ROW

BEGIN

INSERT INTO SalaryLog (EmployeeID, OldSalary, NewSalary, UpdateDate) VALUES (OLD.Employeeld, OLD.Salary, NEW.Salary, NOW());

END;

Use Cases:

• Auditing changes.

• Enforcing business rules.

• Automatically updating related data.

.   .   .

12.3 User-Defined Functions (UDFs)

User-Defined Functions (UDFs):

• Custom functions written by users to perform specific calculations or transformations.

Benefits:

• Reusability.

• Simplifies complex queries.

Example: A UDF to calculate tax:

Sql:

```
CREATE FUNCTION CalculateTax(salary DECIMAL(10, 2))

RETURNS DECIMAL(10, 2)

BEGIN

RETURN salary * 0.15;

END;
```

Usage:

Sql:

SELECT EmployeeID, CalculateTax(Salary) AS Tax FROM Employees;

12.4 Exploring Window Functions

Window Functions:

• Perform calculations across a set of rows related to the current row, without collapsing them into a single result.

Syntax:

Sql:

function() OVER (PARTITION BY column ORDER BY column)

Common Window Functions:

• ROW_NUMBER(): Assigns a unique number to each row.

• RANK(): Provides ranking with ties.

• SUM(), AVG(): Aggregate values over a window.

Example: Rank employees by salary within departments:

Sql:

SELECT EmployeeID, Department, Salary,

RANK() OVER (PARTITION BY Department ORDER BY Salary DESC) AS Rank

FROM Employees;

12.5 Introduction to Common Table Expressions (CTEs)

Common Table Expressions (CTEs):

• A CTE is a temporary result set used within a query.

• **Use Case:** Simplifying complex queries and improving readability.

Syntax:

Sql:

WITH cte_name AS (

SELECT statement

)

SELECT * FROM cte_name;

Example:

Find employees earning above-average salaries:

Sql:

WITH AvgSalary AS (

SELECT Department, AVG(Salary) AS AvgSal

FROM Employees

GROUP BY Department

)

SELECT e.EmployeeID, e.FirstName, e.Salary

FROM Employees e

JOIN AvgSalary a ON e.Department = a.Department

WHERE e.Salary > a.AvgSal;

SQL FOR REAL-WORLD APPLICATIONS

13.1 Connecting SQL with Programming Languages (Python, Java, etc.)

SQL can be integrated with programming languages to make applications dynamic and interactive. Here's how to connect SQL with two common programming languages:

1. Python:

○ Use libraries like sqlite3 for SQLite, MySQL Connector for MySQL, or psycopg2 for PostgreSQL.

Example with SQLite:

Python:

```python
import sqlite3

# Connect to a database

connection = sqlite3.connect('example.db')

cursor = connection.cursor()


# Execute a query

cursor.execute('SELECT * FROM Employees')


# Fetch results

rows = cursor.fetchall()

for row in rows:

print(row)


# Close the connection

connection.close()
```

19 Java:

○ Use JDBC (Java Database Connectivity) to interact with databases.

Example with MySQL:

Java:

import java.sql.*;

public class DatabaseConnection {

public static void main(String[] args) {

try {

// Connect to the database

Connection connection = DriverManager.getConnection(

"jdbc:mysql://localhost:3306/example", "username", "password");

// Execute a query

Statement statement = connection.createStatement();

ResultSet resultSet = statement.executeQuery("SELECT * FROM Employees");

. . .

```
// Process the results

while (resultSet.next()) {

System.out.println(resultSet.getString("FirstName"));

}


// Close the connection

connection.close();

} catch (SQLException e) {

e.printStackTrace();

}

}

}
```

13.2 Building Sample Databases (e.g., E-commerce, Library)

1. E-Commerce Database:

- **Tables:** Products, Orders, Customers, Order-Details.

- **Schema Example:**

Sql:

CREATE TABLE Customers (

CustomerID INT PRIMARY KEY,

CustomerName VARCHAR(100),

Email VARCHAR(100)

);

CREATE TABLE Products (

ProductID INT PRIMARY KEY,

ProductName VARCHAR(100),

Price DECIMAL(10, 2)

);

CREATE TABLE Orders (

OrderID INT PRIMARY KEY,

CustomerID INT,

OrderDate DATE,

```
FOREIGN KEY (CustomerID) REFERENCES
Customers(CustomerID)

);

CREATE TABLE OrderDetails (

OrderDetailID INT PRIMARY KEY,

OrderID INT,

ProductID INT,

Quantity INT,

FOREIGN KEY (OrderID) REFERENCES
Orders(OrderID),

FOREIGN KEY (ProductID) REFERENCES Prod-
ucts(ProductID)

);
```

2. Library Database:

• **Tables:** Books, Members, Loans.

• **Schema Example:**

Sql:

```
CREATE TABLE Books (
```

```sql
BookID INT PRIMARY KEY,

Title VARCHAR(100),

Author VARCHAR(100),

Genre VARCHAR(50)

);

CREATE TABLE Members (

MemberID INT PRIMARY KEY,

MemberName VARCHAR(100),

JoinDate DATE

);

CREATE TABLE Loans (

LoanID INT PRIMARY KEY,

BookID INT,

MemberID INT,

LoanDate DATE,

ReturnDate DATE,

FOREIGN    KEY    (BookID)    REFERENCES
Books(BookID),
```

FOREIGN KEY (MemberID) REFERENCES Members(MemberID)

);

13.3 Automating SQL Queries

Automating SQL queries reduces manual effort and improves efficiency.

1. Using Stored Procedures:

○ Encapsulate queries to execute them automatically with a single call.

Sql:

CREATE PROCEDURE GetRecentOrders()

BEGIN

SELECT * FROM Orders WHERE OrderDate > DATE_SUB(NOW(), INTERVAL 7 DAY);

END;

CALL GetRecentOrders();

9 Scheduling Queries:

○ Use tools like **cron jobs** (Linux) or **SQL Agent** (SQL Server) to schedule query execution.

Example with MySQL Event Scheduler:

Sql:

CREATE EVENT DailyReport

ON SCHEDULE EVERY 1 DAY

DO

INSERT INTO Reports (ReportDate, TotalSales)

SELECT NOW(), SUM(Price * Quantity) FROM OrderDetails;

10 Scripts in Programming Languages:

○ Write Python scripts to automate tasks like data extraction or reporting.

13.4 Data Analysis with SQL

SQL is widely used for analyzing structured data, especially in business intelligence and data science.

1. Aggregation and Summarization:

○ Calculate totals, averages, or counts:

Sql:

SELECT Department, AVG(Salary) AS AvgSalary

FROM Employees

GROUP BY Department;

2. Pivot Tables:

○ Use CASE statements for pivoting data.

Sql:

SELECT

Department,

SUM(CASE WHEN Gender = 'Male' THEN 1 ELSE 0 END) AS MaleEmployees,

SUM(CASE WHEN Gender = 'Female' THEN 1 ELSE 0 END) AS FemaleEmployees

FROM Employees

GROUP BY Department;

· · ·

3. Data Extraction:

○ Use filtering to extract specific insights:

Sql:

SELECT   ProductName,   SUM(Quantity)   AS
TotalSold

FROM OrderDetails

WHERE OrderDate BETWEEN '2024-01-01' AND
'2024-12-31'

GROUP BY ProductName

ORDER BY TotalSold DESC;

4. Integrating with BI Tools:

○ Connect SQL databases to tools like Tableau or
Power BI for visualization and advanced analytics.

14

SECURITY IN SQL

14.1 User Management and Permissions

Proper user management ensures that only autho-
rized individuals have access to specific data and
operations in the database.

Creating Users:

• Use SQL commands to create and manage database users.

• **Example:**

Sql:

CREATE USER 'username'@'localhost' IDENTI-
FIED BY 'password';

. . .

Granting Permissions:

• Grant permissions to allow specific actions on the database.

• **Syntax:**

Sql:

GRANT privilege ON database.table TO 'username'@'host';

• **Examples:**

○ Grant all privileges on a database:

Sql:

GRANT ALL PRIVILEGES ON my_database.* TO 'username'@'localhost';

○ Grant read-only access:

Sql:

GRANT SELECT ON my_database.* TO 'readonly_user'@'localhost';

.   .   .

Revoking Permissions:

• Remove privileges from a user.

Sql:

REVOKE privilege ON database.table FROM 'username'@'host';

Deleting Users:

• Drop a user when it is no longer needed.

Sql:

DROP USER 'username'@'localhost';

14.2 Preventing SQL Injection Attacks

SQL Injection:

• A type of attack where malicious SQL statements are inserted into input fields, potentially giving attackers access to sensitive data.

Prevention Techniques:

1 Use Parameterized Queries (Prepared Statements):

○ Bind variables to placeholders instead of embedding input directly into the query.

Example in Python (MySQL):

Python:

```
cursor.execute("SELECT * FROM Users WHERE username = %s AND password = %s", (username, password))
```

2. Input Validation:

○ Validate and sanitize user inputs to ensure they meet expected formats.

3. Limit Database Privileges:

○ Restrict user accounts to only the permissions they need.

4. Use ORM (Object-Relational Mapping) Tools:

○ Frameworks like SQLAlchemy or Hibernate abstract raw SQL and provide safer ways to interact with databases.

5. Escape Characters:

○ Escape special characters in user input to prevent query manipulation.

. . .

14.3 Encrypting Data in SQL

Encryption in SQL:

• Protects sensitive data by encoding it, so it is accessible only with the proper key.

1. Column-Level Encryption:

○ Encrypt specific columns storing sensitive data.

Example (MySQL):

Sql:

INSERT INTO Users (username, encrypted_-password)

VALUES ('user1', AES_ENCRYPT('mypassword', 'encryption_key'));

2. Decrypt Data:

○ Use the corresponding decryption function to access encrypted data.

Sql:

SELECT AES_DECRYPT(encrypted_password, 'encryption_key') AS password FROM Users;

3. Transport Layer Security (TLS):

○ Encrypt the connection between the application and the database to secure data in transit.

4. Full Disk Encryption:

○ Encrypt the entire database or disk using system-level tools.

Best Practices:

• Store encryption keys securely and separate from the database.

• Regularly rotate encryption keys.

14.4 Auditing and Monitoring SQL Databases

Purpose of Auditing and Monitoring:

• Track user activities and detect unauthorized access or suspicious behavior.

Techniques:

1. Database Audit Logs:

○ Enable logging to record all database operations.

Example (MySQL):

Sql:

SET GLOBAL general_log = 'ON';

2. User Activity Monitoring:

○ Track login attempts, executed queries, and schema changes.

3. Access Control Reports:

○ Generate periodic reports on user privileges and access patterns.

4. Anomaly Detection:

○ Use tools or scripts to detect unusual patterns, such as excessive failed login attempts or large data exports.

5. Third-Party Tools:

○ Tools like **Splunk**, **Datadog**, or **SolarWinds Database Performance Analyzer** provide robust monitoring and alerting capabilities.

Example of Query Logging: Enable query logging to monitor executed queries:

Sql:

SET GLOBAL log_output = 'FILE';

SET   GLOBAL   general_log_file   =
'/var/log/mysql/general.log';

SET GLOBAL general_log = 'ON';

PRACTICAL PROJECTS

15.1 Designing a Simple Blog Database

A blog database requires tables for users, posts, and comments. Below is an example schema:

Schema:

Sql:

CREATE TABLE Users (

UserID INT PRIMARY KEY,

UserName VARCHAR(50),

Email VARCHAR(100)

);

```sql
CREATE TABLE Posts (

PostID INT PRIMARY KEY,

UserID INT,

Title VARCHAR(200),

Content TEXT,

PostDate DATETIME,

FOREIGN KEY (UserID) REFERENCES Users(UserID)

);

CREATE TABLE Comments (

CommentID INT PRIMARY KEY,

PostID INT,

UserID INT,

CommentText TEXT,

CommentDate DATETIME,

FOREIGN KEY (PostID) REFERENCES Posts(PostID),
```

FOREIGN KEY (UserID) REFERENCES Users(UserID)

);

Example Queries:

1. Retrieve all posts with their authors:

Sql:

SELECT Posts.Title, Users.UserName, Posts.-PostDate

FROM Posts

JOIN Users ON Posts.UserID = Users.UserID;

2. Count comments per post:

Sql:

SELECT Posts.Title, COUNT(Comments.CommentID) AS CommentCount

FROM Posts

LEFT JOIN Comments ON Posts.PostID = Comments.PostID

GROUP BY Posts.PostID;

. . .

15.2 Building a Student Management System

A student management system tracks students, courses, and enrollments.

Schema:

Sql:

CREATE TABLE Students (

StudentID INT PRIMARY KEY,

FirstName VARCHAR(50),

LastName VARCHAR(50),

EnrollmentDate DATE

);

CREATE TABLE Courses (

CourseID INT PRIMARY KEY,

CourseName VARCHAR(100),

Credits INT

);

CREATE TABLE Enrollments (

EnrollmentID INT PRIMARY KEY,

StudentID INT,

CourseID INT,

Grade CHAR(2),

FOREIGN KEY (StudentID) REFERENCES Students(StudentID),

FOREIGN KEY (CourseID) REFERENCES Courses(CourseID)

);

Example Queries:

1. List all students enrolled in a specific course:

Sql:

SELECT Students.FirstName, Students.LastName, Courses.CourseName

FROM Enrollments

JOIN Students ON Enrollments.StudentID = Students.StudentID

JOIN Courses ON Enrollments.CourseID = Courses.CourseID

WHERE Courses.CourseName = 'Mathematics';

2. Calculate average grades per course:

Sql:

SELECT   Courses.CourseName,   AVG(CASE WHEN Grade != 'F' THEN Grade END) AS AvgGrade

FROM Enrollments

JOIN Courses ON Enrollments.CourseID = Courses.CourseID

GROUP BY Courses.CourseName;

15.3 Querying a Public Dataset (e.g., COVID-19 data)

Dataset Example: COVID-19 statistics with columns like Country, Date, ConfirmedCases, Deaths, Recovered.

Schema:

Sql:

CREATE TABLE COVID19Stats (

Country VARCHAR(100),

Date DATE,

ConfirmedCases INT,

Deaths INT,

Recovered INT

);

Example Queries:

1. Find the total cases by country:

Sql:

SELECT Country, SUM(ConfirmedCases) AS TotalCases

FROM COVID19Stats

GROUP BY Country

ORDER BY TotalCases DESC;

2. Calculate recovery rate by country:

Sql:

SELECT Country,

SUM(Recovered) / SUM(ConfirmedCases) * 100 AS RecoveryRate

FROM COVID19Stats

GROUP BY Country;

3. Trend analysis for a specific country:

Sql:

SELECT Date, ConfirmedCases, Deaths, Recovered

FROM COVID19Stats

WHERE Country = 'USA'

ORDER BY Date;

15.4 Your First SQL Challenge: Query Optimization

Optimize a query that retrieves top-selling products from an Orders and Products database.

Initial Query:

Sql:

SELECT Products.ProductName, SUM(OrderDetails.Quantity) AS TotalSold

FROM OrderDetails

JOIN Products ON OrderDetails.ProductID = Products.ProductID

GROUP BY Products.ProductName

ORDER BY TotalSold DESC

LIMIT 10;

Optimization Steps:

1. Add Indexes:

○ Index frequently queried columns like OrderDetails.ProductID and Products.ProductID.

Sql:

CREATE INDEX idx_productid ON OrderDetails(ProductID);

2. Avoid Unnecessary Columns:

○ Fetch only required columns to minimize data transfer.

3. Use Query Execution Plan:

○ Analyze execution time to identify bottlenecks.

Sql:

EXPLAIN   SELECT   Products.ProductName, SUM(OrderDetails.Quantity) AS TotalSold

FROM OrderDetails

JOIN   Products   ON   OrderDetails.ProductID   = Products.ProductID

GROUP BY Products.ProductName

ORDER BY TotalSold DESC

LIMIT 10;

ADDITIONAL RESOURCES

16.1 Online SQL Resources and Communities

1. Official Documentation:

○ **MySQL:** dev.mysql.com

○ **PostgreSQL:** postgresql.org/docs

○ **SQLite:** sqlite.org/docs

○ **SQL Server:** docs.microsoft.com/sql

2. Learning Platforms:

○ **W3Schools SQL Tutorial:** Comprehensive beginner-friendly tutorials.

w3schools.com/sql

○ **LeetCode SQL Questions:** Practice SQL queries for real-world scenarios.

leetcode.com/problemset/database

○ **Kaggle:** Datasets and SQL challenges for hands-on practice.

kaggle.com

3. Communities and Forums:

○ **Stack Overflow:** Ask and answer SQL-related questions.

stackoverflow.com

○ **Reddit SQL Community:** Discussions, tips, and problem-solving.

reddit.com/r/SQL

○ **SQLServerCentral:** Resources and discussions specific to SQL Server.

sqlservercentral.com

4. Online Courses:

○ **Coursera SQL Specializations:** Courses from universities and industry experts.

○ **Udemy SQL Courses:** Affordable courses with lifetime access.

○ **DataCamp SQL:** Interactive SQL training with practical projects.

16.2 Popular SQL Tools and Extensions

1. Database Management Tools:

○ **MySQL Workbench:** GUI for designing and managing MySQL databases.

○ **pgAdmin:** PostgreSQL administration and management.

○ **SQL Server Management Studio (SSMS):** Advanced tool for SQL Server.

2. SQL Query Editors:

○ **DBeaver:** Universal database management tool supporting multiple databases.

○ **DataGrip:** JetBrains' tool for advanced SQL querying and database management.

3. Extensions for Advanced Features:

○ **PostGIS:** Geospatial extensions for PostgreSQL.

○ **JSON Functions (MySQL/PostgreSQL):** Handle and query JSON data directly in SQL.

○ **Oracle SQL Developer:** Comprehensive tool for Oracle Database.

4. Visualization Tools:

○ **Tableau:** SQL-powered dashboards and visual analytics.

○ **Power BI:** Interactive reporting with SQL integration.

16.3 Sample SQL Certifications to Explore

1. Vendor-Specific Certifications:

○ **Oracle Database SQL Certified Associate:** Validate foundational SQL skills.

○ **Microsoft Certified: Azure Data Fundamentals:** Focuses on SQL in Azure environments.

○ **MySQL Developer Certification:** For advanced MySQL expertise.

2. General Certifications:

o **IBM Data Science Professional Certificate:** SQL is a core component.

o **Google Data Analytics Professional Certificate:** Covers SQL for analysis tasks.

3. Free Certifications:

o **Kaggle SQL Micro-Courses:** Short courses with certification of completion.

o **Mode Analytics SQL Tutorial and Certificate:** Hands-on SQL learning.

4. Advanced Certifications:

o **Certified Business Intelligence Professional (CBIP):** SQL for data analysis.

o **PostgreSQL Certified Developer:** Focus on PostgreSQL-specific capabilities.

16.4 Glossary of Key SQL Terms

DDL: Data Definition Language; commands like CREATE, ALTER, DROP.

DML: Data Manipulation Language; commands like SELECT, INSERT, UPDATE, DELETE.

Primary Key: A unique identifier for each record in a table.

Foreign Key: A field in one table that links to the primary key in another table.

Join: Combines rows from two or more tables based on a related column.

Index: A database object that improves query performance by enabling faster lookups.

View: A virtual table based on the result of a SQL query.

Stored Procedure: A precompiled collection of SQL statements stored in the database.

Transaction: A sequence of operations executed as a single unit of work.

Normalization: Process of organizing data to minimize redundancy and improve integrity.

Subquery: A query nested inside another query.

17

CONCLUSION

17.1 Recap of Key Concepts

This book has covered the fundamental and advanced concepts of SQL, equipping you with the knowledge to effectively interact with relational databases. Here's a summary of the key topics:

1. Introduction to SQL:

○ Basics of SQL syntax and its importance in managing structured data.

2. Working with Databases:

○ Understanding tables, rows, columns, and relationships (one-to-one, one-to-many, many-to-many).

3. Querying Data:

○   Using SELECT, WHERE, ORDER BY, and LIMIT for efficient data retrieval.

4. Data Manipulation:

○   Adding, updating, and deleting data with INSERT, UPDATE, and DELETE.

5. Advanced Querying:

○   Aggregate functions (COUNT, SUM, AVG), GROUP BY, HAVING, joins, and subqueries.

6. Database Design and Management:

○   Creating tables, defining constraints (NOT NULL, UNIQUE, PRIMARY KEY, FOREIGN KEY), and maintaining data integrity.

7. Performance Optimization:

○   Using indexes and query optimization techniques.

8. Advanced Features:

○ Stored procedures, triggers, window functions, and Common Table Expressions (CTEs).

9. Security and Real-World Applications:

○ User management, preventing SQL injection, and integrating SQL with programming languages like Python and Java.

17.2 Next Steps in Your SQL Journey

1. Practice Real-World Projects:

○ Create sample databases for scenarios like e-commerce, student management, or blogging platforms.

○ Explore open datasets (e.g., COVID-19 statistics, financial records) for hands-on analysis.

2. Explore Advanced Topics:

○ Learn about database replication, sharding, and distributed databases.

○ Dive into NoSQL databases like MongoDB for unstructured data.

3. Certifications and Specializations:

○ Pursue SQL certifications (e.g., Oracle, Microsoft, PostgreSQL) to validate your skills.

○ Explore data science or business intelligence specializations that integrate SQL.

4. Collaborate and Contribute:

○ Join online communities like Stack Overflow, Reddit, and Kaggle to solve challenges and share knowledge.

5. Integrate with Tools:

○ Use SQL alongside BI tools (Tableau, Power BI) or integrate it into applications using programming languages.

17.3 Encouragement to Keep Practicing

SQL is a skill that grows stronger with consistent practice. As you work on real-world problems, you'll uncover creative ways to solve complex challenges. Remember:

• Start small but think big—master the fundamentals and gradually explore advanced concepts.

• Don't fear mistakes; each error is a stepping stone toward mastery.

• The demand for SQL skills spans every industry, making your expertise valuable and versatile.

Quote to Inspire:

"Practice does not make perfect. Only perfect practice makes perfect." – Vince Lombardi

With your foundation in SQL, the possibilities are endless. Keep practicing, stay curious, and let SQL unlock the potential of your data!

www.ingramcontent.com/pod-product-compliance
Lightning Source LLC
LaVergne TN
LVHW051344050326
832903LV00031B/3732